YOUR KNOWLEDGE HAS VALUE

- We will publish your bachelor's and master's thesis, essays and papers

- Your own eBook and book - sold worldwide in all relevant shops

- Earn money with each sale

Upload your text at www.GRIN.com and publish for free

Bibliographic information published by the German National Library:

The German National Library lists this publication in the National Bibliography; detailed bibliographic data are available on the Internet at http://dnb.dnb.de .

This book is copyright material and must not be copied, reproduced, transferred, distributed, leased, licensed or publicly performed or used in any way except as specifically permitted in writing by the publishers, as allowed under the terms and conditions under which it was purchased or as strictly permitted by applicable copyright law. Any unauthorized distribution or use of this text may be a direct infringement of the author s and publisher s rights and those responsible may be liable in law accordingly.

Imprint:

Copyright © 2016 GRIN Verlag, Open Publishing GmbH
Print and binding: Books on Demand GmbH, Norderstedt Germany
ISBN: 9783668614352

This book at GRIN:

https://www.grin.com/document/387033

Dalien Tru

Trump and the media

GRIN Publishing

GRIN - Your knowledge has value

Since its foundation in 1998, GRIN has specialized in publishing academic texts by students, college teachers and other academics as e-book and printed book. The website www.grin.com is an ideal platform for presenting term papers, final papers, scientific essays, dissertations and specialist books.

Visit us on the internet:

http://www.grin.com/

http://www.facebook.com/grincom

http://www.twitter.com/grin_com

Trump
and the media

1. What happened?

It was June the 16th, 2015, when Donald Junior Trump, a nationwide known American businessman, formally announced his candidacy for the United States presidential election of 2016. At Trump Tower in New York City, firstly being introduced by his daughter Ivanca Trump as „a man, who needs no introduction"[1], he ascended a small podium in front of the middle-sized croud and after cross-referencing about ISIS, the foreign policies of China, Japan and Mexico, the current economic situation of the USA and Obamacare he finally spoke the *magic* words: „I am officially running (…) for president of the United States"[2].

The annoucement was followed by an endless series of amused comments, articles in the media and statements from fellow party members regarding Trump and his intentions. Virtually no established media attributed Trump a chance to win the race for the nomination. The Chicago Tribune for instance saw no „serious chance of winning" for Trump[3], along the way The Guardian listed all the reasons on „why Donald Trump won't win the Republican presidential nomination"[4]. Altough many media recognized the fact that Trump in the following months had a good standing in most polls they doubted that he could affectively transfer his advance in the surveys into long-term electoral successes. Even *FiveThirthyEight*, a website that is engaged with opinion poll analysis and is best known for correctly predicting the vote winner of all 50 states in the 2012 presidential election, climbed on the bandwagon and stated Trump indeed „winning the polls"[5], but „losing the nomination"[6]. In short: Trump were attributed no serious chances to win the nomination and his ambitions were mostly seen as a joke.

During the following months, though, the until there unthinkable became a reality. Week after week and primary after primary he forged ahead to the republican candidates field. Trump was the candidate, who got more primary votes than any other Republican in the history of USA – accumulating 13,4 million votes and consequently relegating Bushs 12,1 million votes in the 2000 primaries to the second place[7]. As a result Trump officially became the Republican Party's presidential nominee for the presidential election of 2016.

In the light of this development – from the initial commonly shared sight of Trump's candi-

---

1 https://www.youtube.com/watch?v=q_q61B-DyPk [accessed on 30.09.16]
2 http://time.com/3923128/donald-trump-announcement-speech/ [accessed on 30.09.16]
3 http://www.chicagotribune.com/news/nationworld/ [accessed on 30.09.16]
4 https://www.theguardian.com/us-news/2015/aug/22/donald-trump-wont-win-republican-presidential-nomination [accessed on 30.09.16]
5 http://fivethirtyeight.com/datalab/donald-trump-is-winning-the-polls-and-losing-the-nomination/ [accessed on 30.09.16]
6 Ibid.
7 https://www.theatlas.com/charts/HJucYAHE [accessed on 30.09.16]

dacy as a foremost clownish one to his landslide victory of the Republican Party presidential primaries – and within the framework of this essay the following question arises:
Which factors lead to Trumps victories in the Republican Party presidential primaries and the following GOP presidential nomination in 2016?

2. Why did it happen?

To understand Trump's victory of the Republican Party presidential primaries to the core an accurate reflection on the sourrounding field of his former competitors is indispensable. To begin with there has to be considered the quantity of the other Republican candidates: Starting with Ted Cruz, Senator of Texas, the former Governor of Florida Jeb Bush, the Senator Marco Rubio of Florida up to the Governor of Ohio, John Kasich – just to name a few – all in all and besides Trump there were 16 major candidates for the race. This was a record in the number of presidential candidates for any political party in American history[8]. The pattern of this field on its own, in which Trump was not constrained to be confronted with a compact field of candidates but instead as luck would have it was located inbetween a shattered group of many contestants, can be seen as one factor that lead to Trump's nomination.

Additional to the fragmented structure in the aggregate not one of Trumps competitors could be described as a distuingished appearance[9]. The former governor Jeb Bush, for example, who in comparison to the other candidates invested by far the highest amount of money into presidential ads during his campaign – in numbers: 82 million dollars[10] – was mostly perceived as an unflattering candidate both by the media and the public. Symptomatic for this widely shared viewpoint is the fact that in 2015 his campaign team missed out on purchasing the website *JebBush.com*, so that visitors of the site were redirected to the Trump's campaign website[11]. Another of Trumps competitors, Senator Marco Rubio, was characterized as a dreary candidate, having one of his most reported moments during the Republican Party presidential primaries at a debate in New Hampshire in which he repeated the same line about the in his opinion ongoing attempt Obamas to change the USA in a negative way for four (!) times[12].

In the first sight all of the above mentioned constellations – the internal structure of the field

---

8 http://time.com/3948922/jim-gilmore-virginia-2016/ [accessed on 30.09.16]
9 http://www.usnews.com/opinion/blogs/lara-brown/2015/08/31/gops-2016-problem-isnt-trump-its-everybody-else [accessed on 30.09.16]
10 http://www.nytimes.com/2016/03/16/upshot/measuring-donald-trumps-mammoth-advantage-in-free-media.html?_r=2 [accessed on 30.09.16]
11 https://www.washingtonpost.com/news/morning-mix/wp/2016/02/17/jebbush-com-redirects-to-trumps-site-but-wait-till-you-see-where-tedcruzforamerica-com-goes/ [accessed on 30.09.16]
12 http://time.com/4210991/marco-rubio-gop-debate-new-hampshire/ [accessed on 30.09.16]

of the Republican candidates and their individual weaknesses – are not necesserely implicating an advantage for Trump, but on closer inspection the interplay of the factors play into the hands of Trump. Firstly there is the high number of candidates: Trump, long before announcing his participation in the presidential race and stepping into the political sphere, was already playing a part in the public sphere. As a businessman, author and co-producer of his own tv-show „The Apprentice" – broadcasted on NBC – Trump was yet well-known to a broad audience[13]. In the light of his degree of popularity the highly fragmented field of republican candidates was fitting perfectly into Trumps election battle and can be seen as one basic factor for Trumps victories in the primaries and his nomination. Secondly to the individual competitors of Trump and their weak points: Trump is infamously noted for his aggressive behaviour towards rivals, previously mainly in the economic field and in a more tabloid-character like way in his former television appearances. The New York Times enumerates a total of 258 people, places and things Trump has insulted since his declaration for his candidacy for president – counting only the offences published on his twitter-account[14]. Amongst those insults resided many that were directly aimed at the chinks of his political opponents. Trumps „specialty" in this connection was his ability for creating as simple as offending name callings: *Lyin' Ted*, *low-energy Jeb* and *little Marco* are just three of his many incidences that evolved into largely recognizable known winged words and with permanent repetition began to assign to the adressed competitors – even if the ascriptions were not slighty tied to (their) real conditions[15]. The GOP field that – even aside from Trump and his rally – could be characterized by a number of prevailingly weak candidates and it's clash with Trumps ability to pick up on their weak points while meanwhile escalating himself could be named as another factor that lead to Trump's nomination.

Aside of the internal structure of the candidates field on the GOP side there is also a factor that could be described as a macro-level explanation for Trump's nomination. With the 2008 election of Barack Obama as president the Tea Party movement began to arise[16]. A driven force of the grassroots movement was the activation of „racial fears and resentments"[17] due to Obamas presidency as the first black president. One in the movement widespread theory asserts Obama to not being born in the United States and secretly being a Muslim[18]. Till the present the Tea Party can be considered as a influential force in the GOP and among its party-electorate. Altough some of the other Republican candidates – among those Ted Cruz – had strong ties to the movement, Trump was the

---

13 http://www.deutschlandfunk.de/portraet-das-phaenomen-donald-trump.1818.de.html?dram:article_id=354070 [accessed on 30.09.16]
14 http://www.nytimes.com/interactive/2016/01/28/upshot/donald-trump-twitter-insults.html [accessed on 30.09.16]
15 https://www.washingtonpost.com/news/inspired-life/wp/2016/04/20/little-marco-lying-ted-crooked-hillary-donald-trumps-winning-strategy-nouns/ [accessed on 30.09.16]
16 Abramowitz, Grand Old Tea Party. Partisan Polarization and the Rise of the Tea Party Movement, p. 197.
17 Ibid.
18 Abramowitz, Grand Old Tea Party. Partisan Polarization and the Rise of the Tea Party Movement, p. 198.

only one embracing some of the Tea Partys most radical positions by publicly doubting the authenticity of Obamas birth certificate[19] and expressing the wish to ban all Muslims from entering the United States[20]. In doing so he was securing the backing and votes of this movement.

One generally not in the first place mentioned factor for Trumps victories in the Republican Party presidential primaries and caucuses – and therein lies the core-issue of this essay – can be found in the media coverage of Trump and his election campaign. Before misconceptions arise: The term of media coverage in the context of this essay refers primer to the US-american media landscape. In its structure it consists of 1800 television stations, 10.000 daily and weekly newspapers and 15.000 radio stations that emit nonstop information in the United States, in which on the big five media corporations – Time Warner, Disney, Murdoch´s News Corporation, General Electric/NBC und CBS Corp. – control over 90% of the US-market[21]. The US-american media landscape therefore can be described as a highly privatized and capitalistic one.

From the very first moment of Trumps campaign on – beginning with his presidential annoucement speech – every single one of his actions and comments was registered and reproduced by and in the media. Indeed, in his annoucement speech Trump claimed that people were being send from Mexico to the United States while „bringing drugs, … bringing crime"[22] and being „rapists"[23]. This insults dominated the headlines for many days. As it was the very first of Trumps numerous claims as a political figure it is comprehensible that the media picked up the topic, but instead of depicting the ridiculousness of the contention in a critical manner and thereby debunking Trumps words as what they were – absurd and abusive claims – the media repeated the event over and over again in an attention-grabbing way and only hyped it by doing so. Altough this was the first one of Trump's – some say well-thought-out – taboo-brakes, all of the numerous following ones took their course in the same patterns.

At this juncture it is important to mention that the described omnipresence of Trump in the media is not resulting from a subjective viewpoint or feeling, but can be condensed in hard numbers: medianQuant, a company that among other things seeked the media coverage of the Republican candidates and calculates their dollar merit, came to the conclusion that Trump, in the time period from his annoucement speech to march 2016, got an amount of earned media – comments and news on him or his campaign, for which he had to pay nothing – equivalent to nearly 2 billion dol-

---

19 http://www.huffingtonpost.com/2015/02/27/donald-trump-cpac_n_6756836.html [accessed on 30.09.16]
20 https://www.washingtonpost.com/politics/trump-pushes-expanded-ban-on-muslims-and-other-foreigners/2016/06/13/c9988e96-317d-11e6-8ff7-7b6c1998b7a0_story.html [accessed on 30.09.16]
21 http://www.bpb.de/internationales/amerika/usa/10707/medien-in-den-usa [accessed on 30.09.16]
22 http://edition.cnn.com/2015/06/17/opinions/kohn-donald-trump-announcement/ [accessed on 30.09.16
23 Ibid.

lars[24]. The added free media value of the following 13 (!) Republican candidates – from Ted Cruz with 313 million dollars, followed by Jeb Bush with 214 and Marco Rubio with 204 up to Bobby Jindal with 7 million dollars – is around 1,16 billion dollars and does not even come close to Trumps account[25]. The mainstream media could be described as a resonant sphere to Trumps statements, under whom a numerous amount of racist, anti-feminist and plain false claims can be found. The steady dissemination of Trumps statements can be seen as a central – if not *the* central – factor that lead to his victories in the primaries and the following nomination.

According to Pierre Bourdieu, a 2002 deceased french intellectual, who had a lifelong dispute on political issues, this manner of the american media landscape follows an intrasystem logic. In his book *On Television* (original: *Sur la télévision*) Bourdieu refers – explicitly – on „die tausend pathologischen Züge des amerikanischen Fernsehens [the thousand pathological characteristics of the US-american television landscape]"[26] and expatiates the capitalistic structure of the private television. From this pattern it follows that the goal of reports, shows, comments and the news is to generate audience and with it money. In fact the *relationship* between Trump and the media is not a unilateral one. As shown, the media is willing to give Trump an enormous amount of free broadcasting time, but on the other hand the media conglomerates profit from every minute they broadcast anything about Trump and his campaign. The first Republican primary debate on August the 6th 2015, when Trump presented himself for the first time as a political protagonist, bestowed the conservative television transmitter *Fox News* the highest viewing rate in the history of the channel and – aside from sporting events – the all the time highest rate in U.S. cable television at all[27].

In other words and from the perspective of the media: With Trumps comes audience and the audience brings the money. In the media business one is very aware of this fact, as the following statement from Leslie Moonves, Chairman of CBS, shows: At the Morgan Stanley Technology, Media & Telecom Conference in San Francisco he announced that Trump's candidacy „may not be good for America, but it's damn good for CBS (…). The money's rolling in and this is fun. I've never seen anything like this, and this is going to be a very good year for us. Sorry. It's a terrible thing to say. But, bring it on, Donald. Keep going."[28]

Another effect of the logic of profit in the field of the media according to Bourdieu leads to the „zirkuläre Zirkulation der Nachricht [circular circulation of the news]"[29]. To follow the impetus

---

24 http://www.nytimes.com/2016/03/16/upshot/measuring-donald-trumps-mammoth-advantage-in-free-media.html?_r=2 [accessed on 30.09.16]
25 Ibid.
26 Bourdieu, Pierre, Über das Fernsehen, Frankfurt am Main, 1989, p. 10.
27 https://www.washingtonpost.com/news/the-fix/wp/2015/08/07/24-million-people-watched-the-trump-debate-thats-a-record-by-a-lot/ [accessed on 30.09.16]
28 http://www.politico.com/blogs/on-media/2016/02/les-moonves-trump-cbs-220001 [accessed on 30.09.16]
29 Bourdieu, Über das Fernsehen, p. 30ff.

of the viewing rate and the money making media corporations either have to land a coup or – and this is the much more easy path – they go for an approved report, which promises interest and attention – in fine and other words: rate and money. The medial coverage on Trump shows this perfectly: time and time again the media leaped up on one of Trumps statements, reporting what other media refered on Trump, continuing with the reaction of one of the *other candidates* – this commonly used term by oneself shows what an outstanding role Trump was conceded by the media in the race – to his statements before continuing to ask Trump himself on the caused reactions of his previous comment – the circular circulation of the *trumpish* news seemed to be brought to perfection.

Furthermore Bourdieu shows that in the field of television the role-model of the so-called „fast-thinkers"[30] as a person who can give fast answers in form of platitudes to every current topic. Trump can be seen as an embodiment of this figure: In October 2015 the language complexity of all 19 presidential candidates was examined and the result showed that Trump used by far the most simple language – allowing a 4th grade scholar to follow his words without difficulty[31].

At this point there has been shown proof for the tremendous media presence of Trump and the fitting accuracy with which the intrasystem logic of the media sphere and Trump fit in another. But most of the media coverage about Trump seemed to let him appear in a bad light – why should the extensive recording therefore be critized as an constant impulse for Trumps election battle? It seems that yet another time Trump must be seen as an particular case capable of internalizing the *there is no such thing as bad publicity* mantra and managing to leverage the little complimentary coverage. As a matter of fact the american political scientist John Sides proved evidence in several accounts that there is a direct link between the coverage Trump gets in the media and his poll ratings[32]. Under consideration of this connection the media coverage on Trump and his campaign can be clearly identified as a major cause for Trumps victories in the primaries and his nomination.

3. What's going to happen?

In summary it can be said that Trump's victories in the primaries and his subsequent presidential nomination as a multicausal outcome is caused by several factors. Surely the structure of Trumps competitors field and the weaknesses of his individual concurrents here are not to be neglected. For the

---

30 Bourdieu, Über das Fernsehen, p. 39.
31 http://www.bostonglobe.com/news/politics/2015/10/20/donald-trump-and-ben-carson-speak-grade-school-level-that-today-voters-can-quickly-grasp/LUCBY6uwQAxiLvvXbVTSUN/story.html [accessed on 30.09.16]
32 https://www.washingtonpost.com/blogs/monkey-cage/wp/2015/07/20/why-is-trump-surging-blame-the-media/ [accessed on 30.09.16] and https://www.washingtonpost.com/blogs/monkey-cage/wp/2015/08/28/why-does-trump-remain-atop-the-polls-you-can-still-blame-the-media/ [accessed on 30.09.16] and https://www.washingtonpost.com/blogs/monkey-cage/wp/2015/09/16/can-we-stop-blaming-the-media-for-donald-trump-nope-not-at-all/ [accessed on 30.09.16]

explanation of further factors the macroscopic viewpoint that takes the radical anti-Obama mood of the Tea Party movement in conjunction with Trumps thereby suitable points of view into consideration plays a role too.

The central factor however seems to lay within the media sphere. The steady medial impetus to generate profits appears in the processes of the *circular circulation of information*[33] and the need for an easy accessable *fast-thinker*[34]. Due to this intrasystem logics the mainstream media constatly records and reproduces Trumps numerous statements – in other words: Trump is in the news, because every news with Trump generates audience and therefore money. The above-average reporting on Trump and his diverse statements in the media – especially in comparison to his political opponents – has as well be shown as the intense effects of this medial omnipresence on the polls and results of the primaries.

It's going to be November the 8th, 2016, when the presidential elections are going to take place. Meanwhile and after Donald Trumps nomination the media seems to have taken a more self-critical perspective on the affirmative effects their coverage unfolded on Trumps campaign. By all required scientific neutrality there remains the hope that the rethinking process in the media sphere doesn't contribute to advance Trump in the White House but instead helps to preserve and strengthen the universal values of humanity and respect, that have already been affected too many times by Donald Junior Trump.

---

33 Bourdieu, Über das Fernsehen, p. 30ff.
34 Bourdieu, Über das Fernsehen, p. 39.

Bibliography

Abramowitz, Alan I. (2012), *Grand Old Tea Party. Partisan Polarization and the Rise of the Tea Party Movement*, in: Rosenthal, Lawrence/Christine, Trost (Ed.), Steep. The Precipitous Rise of the Tea Party, California, p. 195-211.

Bourdieu, Pierre (1989), *Über das Fernsehen*, Frankfurt am Main.

Internet Sources

https://www.youtube.com/watch?v=q_q61B-DyPk [accessed on 30.09.16]

http://time.com/3923128/donald-trump-announcement-speech/ [accessed on 30.09.16]

http://www.chicagotribune.com/news/nationworld/ [accessed on 30.09.16]

https://www.theguardian.com/us-news/2015/aug/22/donald-trump-wont-win-republican-presidential-nomination [accessed on 30.09.16]

http://fivethirtyeight.com/datalab/donald-trump-is-winning-the-polls-and-losing-the-nomination/ [accessed on 30.09.16]

https://www.theatlas.com/charts/HJucYAHE [accessed on 30.09.16]

http://time.com/3948922/jim-gilmore-virginia-2016/ [accessed on 30.09.16]

http://www.usnews.com/opinion/blogs/lara-brown/2015/08/31/gops-2016-problem-isnt-trump-its-everybody-else [accessed on 30.09.16]

http://www.nytimes.com/2016/03/16/upshot/measuring-donald-trumps-mammoth-advantage-in-free-media.html?_r=2 [accessed on 30.09.16]

https://www.washingtonpost.com/news/morning-mix/wp/2016/02/17/jebbush-com-redirects-to-trumps-site-but-wait-till-you-see-where-tedcruzforamerica-com-goes/ [accessed on 30.09.16]

http://time.com/4210991/marco-rubio-gop-debate-new-hampshire/ [accessed on 30.09.16]

http://www.deutschlandfunk.de/portraet-das-phaenomen-donald-trump.1818.de.html?dram:article_id=354070 [accessed on 30.09.16]

http://www.nytimes.com/interactive/2016/01/28/upshot/donald-trump-twitter-insults.html [accessed on 30.09.16]

https://www.washingtonpost.com/news/inspired-life/wp/2016/04/20/little-marco-lying-ted-crooked-hillary-donald-trumps-winning-strategy-nouns/ [accessed on 30.09.16]

http://www.huffingtonpost.com/2015/02/27/donald-trump-cpac_n_6756805.html [accessed on 30.09.16]

https://www.washingtonpost.com/politics/trump-pushes-expanded-ban-on-muslims-and-other-foreigners/2016/06/13/c9988e96-317d-11e6-8ff7-7b6c1998b7a0_story.html [accessed on 30.09.16]

http://www.bpb.de/internationales/amerika/usa/10707/medien-in-den-usa [accessed on 30.09.16]

http://edition.cnn.com/2015/06/17/opinions/kohn-donald-trump-announcement/ [accessed on 30.09.16

http://www.nytimes.com/2016/03/16/upshot/measuring-donald-trumps-mammoth-advantage-in-free-media.html?_r=2 [accessed on 30.09.16]

https://www.washingtonpost.com/news/the-fix/wp/2015/08/07/24-million-people-watched-the-trump-debate-thats-a-record-by-a-lot/ [accessed on 30.09.16]

http://www.politico.com/blogs/on-media/2016/02/les-moonves-trump-cbs-220001 [accessed on 30.09.16]

http://www.bostonglobe.com/news/politics/2015/10/30/donald-trump-and-ben-carson-speak-grade-school-level-that-today-voters-can-quickly-grasp/LUCBY6uwQAxiLvvXbVTSUN/story.html [accessed on 30.09.16]

https://www.washingtonpost.com/blogs/monkey-cage/wp/2015/07/20/why-is-trump-surging-blame-the-media/ [accessed on 30.09.16]

https://www.washingtonpost.com/blogs/monkey-cage/wp/2015/08/28/why-does-trump-remain-atop-the-polls-you-can-still-blame-the-media/ [accessed on 30.09.16]

https://www.washingtonpost.com/blogs/monkey-cage/wp/2015/09/16/can-we-stop-blaming-the-media-for-donald-trump-nope-not-at-all/ [accessed on 30.09.16]

YOUR KNOWLEDGE HAS VALUE

- We will publish your bachelor's and master's thesis, essays and papers

- Your own eBook and book - sold worldwide in all relevant shops

- Earn money with each sale

Upload your text at www.GRIN.com
and publish for free